Jr. Graphic Colonial America

The Life of a Colonial Schoolteacher

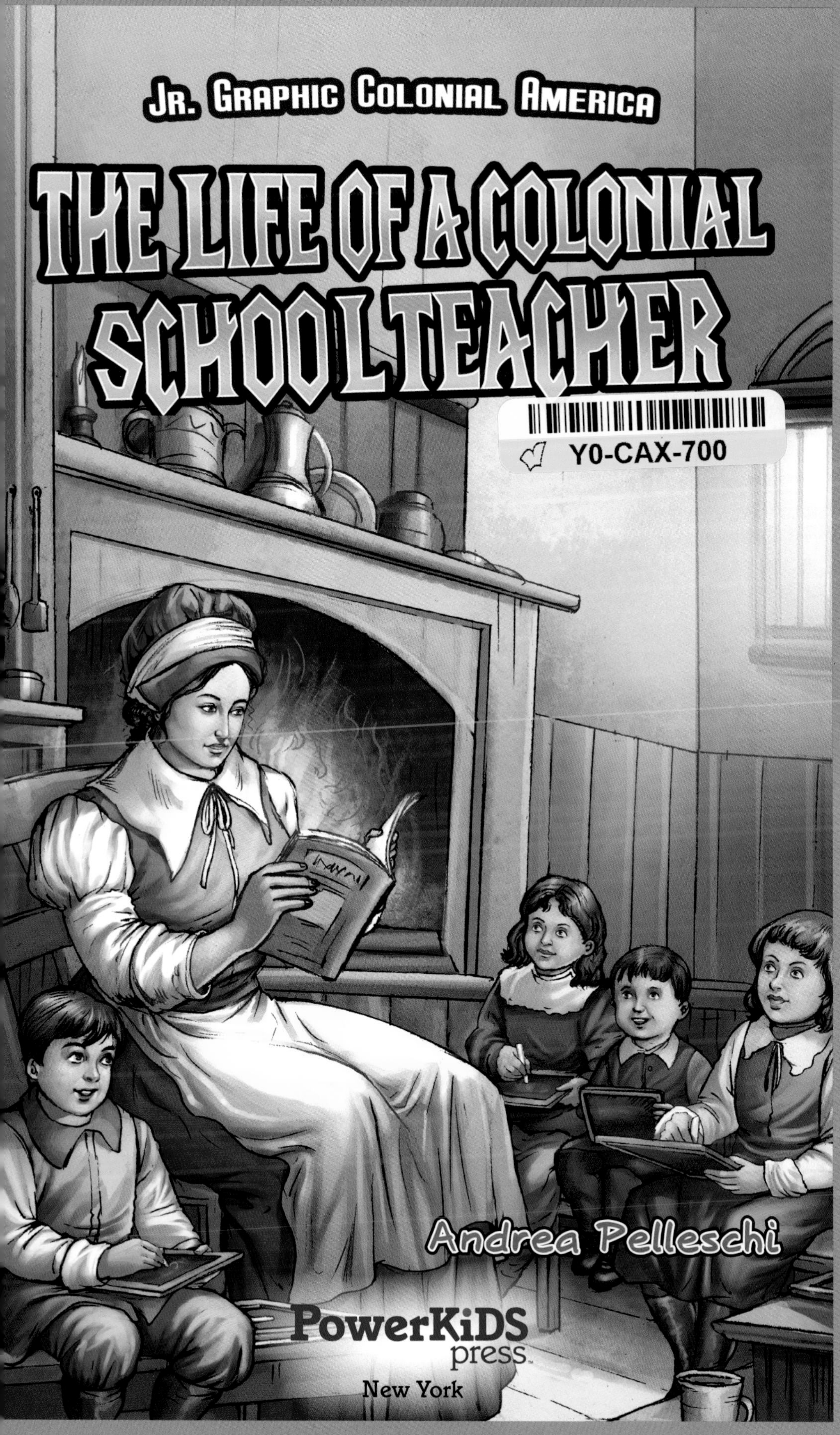

Andrea Pelleschi

PowerKiDS press
New York

Published in 2014 by The Rosen Publishing Group, Inc.
29 East 21st Street, New York, NY 10010

Note: The main characters in this book were real-life colonists who held the jobs described. In some cases, not much else is known about their lives. When necessary, we have used the best available historical scholarship on the professions and daily life in colonial America to create as full and accurate a portrayal as possible.

First Edition

Editor: Joanne Randolph
Book Design: Planman Technologies
Illustrations: Planman Technologies

Library of Congress Cataloging-in-Publication Data

Pelleschi, Andrea.
The life of a colonial schoolteacher / by Andrea Pelleschi.
   p. cm. -- (Jr. graphic colonial America)
Includes index.
ISBN 978-1-4777-1305-1 (library binding) -- ISBN 978-1-4777-1427-0 (pbk.) -- ISBN 978-1-4777-1428-7 (6-pack)
1. Education -- United States -- History -- Juvenile literature. 2. United States -- History -- Colonial period, ca. 1600-1775 -- Juvenile literature. 3. United States -- Social life and customs -- To 1775 -- Juvenile literature. I. Pelleschi, Andrea, 1962- II. Title.
LA206.P45 2014
973.2--dc23

Manufactured in the United States of America

CPSIA Compliance Information: Batch #S13PK1: For Further Information contact Rosen Publishing, New York, New York at 1-800-237-9932

CONTENTS

Introduction   3

Main Characters   3

The Life of a Colonial Schoolteacher   4

Famous Colonial Schoolteachers   22

Glossary   23

Index and Websites   24

INTRODUCTION

In Colonial America, young children were taught at home by a parent or **tutor**, or they attended a dame school. Run by women out of their homes, dame schools taught children ages two to seven the basics of reading, writing, and arithmetic. After attending a dame school, boys either went into an **apprenticeship** to learn a trade, such as cabinetmaking, or they went to a grammar school, where they studied Latin and Greek in preparation for university. Because girls were expected to get married and raise families, they did not go to school after the dame school. However, some girls were apprenticed to an older woman who taught them the art of "housewifery."

MAIN CHARACTERS

Mrs. Neill A dame schoolteacher. Mrs. Neill taught children ages two to seven in her home for a few coins per student.

Sarah and Charles Six-year-old Sarah attends the dame school with her brother, Charles, who is four. Sarah is working on a **sampler** with Mrs. Neill.

Luke and Josiah Seven-year-old Luke attends school with his brother, Josiah, who is six. Luke will soon be old enough to move on to a grammar school.

Anne and Beth Five-year-old Anne attends school with her sister Beth, who is still a toddler.

The Life of a Colonial Schoolteacher

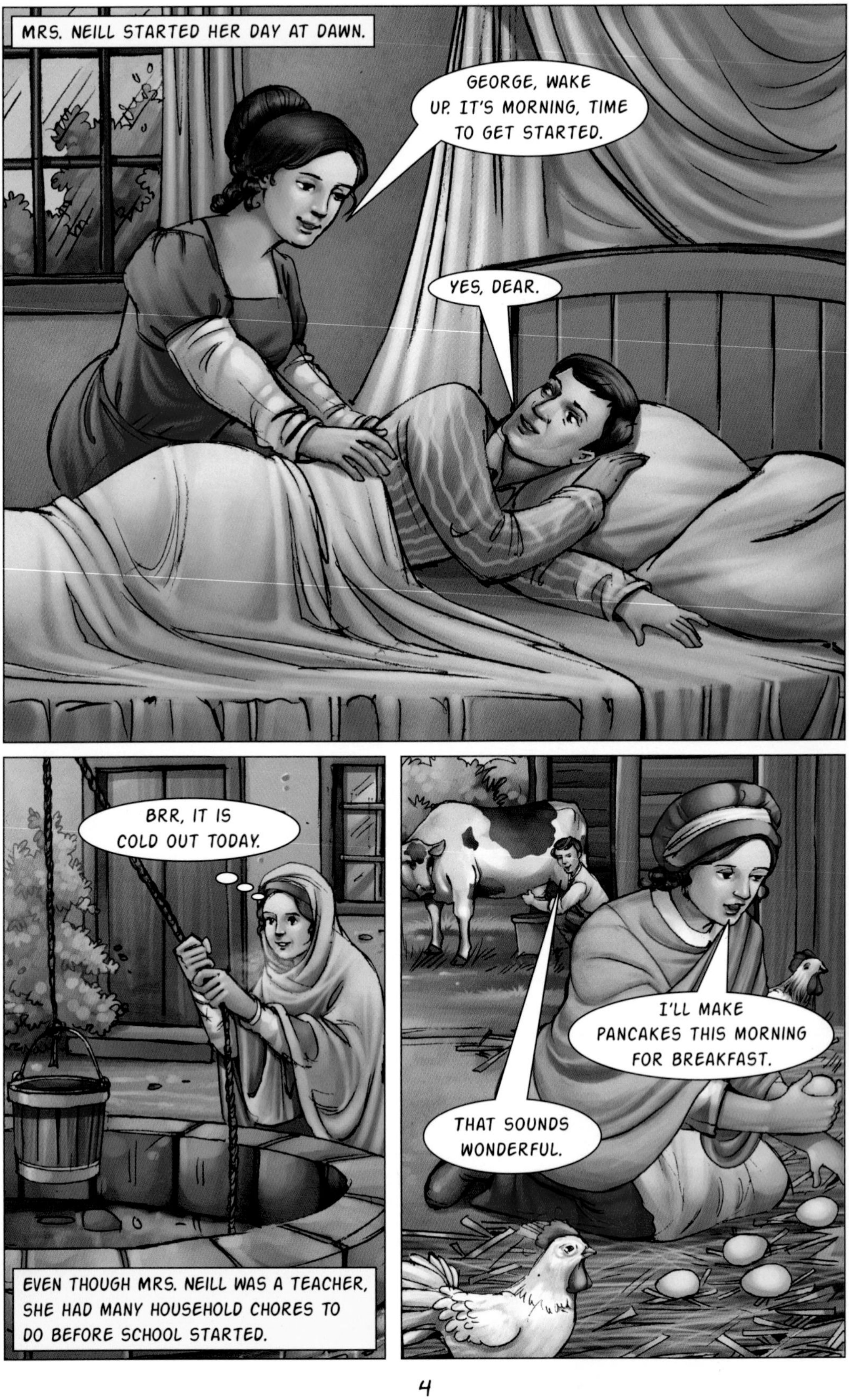
MRS. NEILL STARTED HER DAY AT DAWN.
GEORGE, WAKE UP. IT'S MORNING, TIME TO GET STARTED.
YES, DEAR.
BRR, IT IS COLD OUT TODAY.
EVEN THOUGH MRS. NEILL WAS A TEACHER, SHE HAD MANY HOUSEHOLD CHORES TO DO BEFORE SCHOOL STARTED.
I'LL MAKE PANCAKES THIS MORNING FOR BREAKFAST.
THAT SOUNDS WONDERFUL.

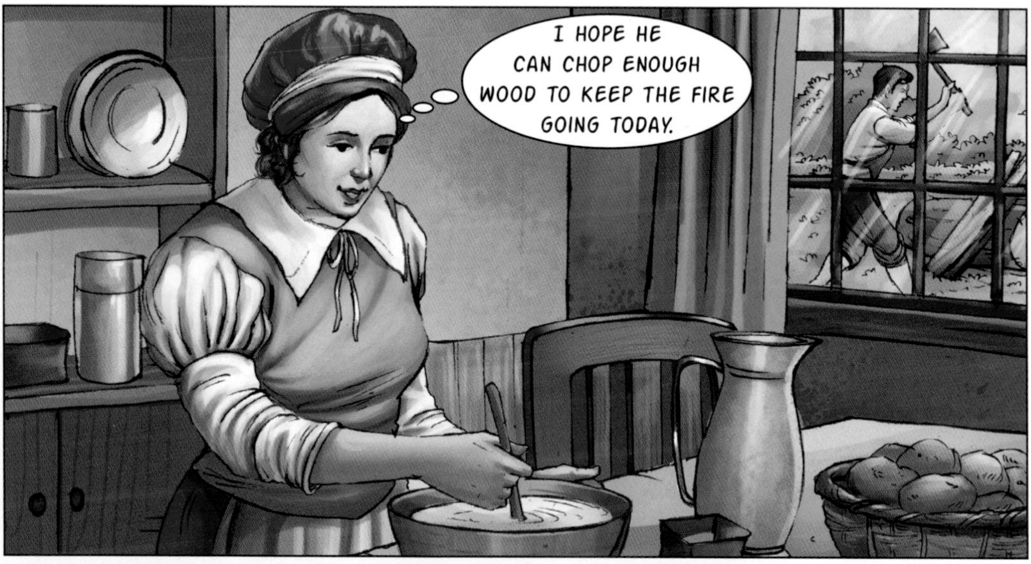
I HOPE HE CAN CHOP ENOUGH WOOD TO KEEP THE FIRE GOING TODAY.

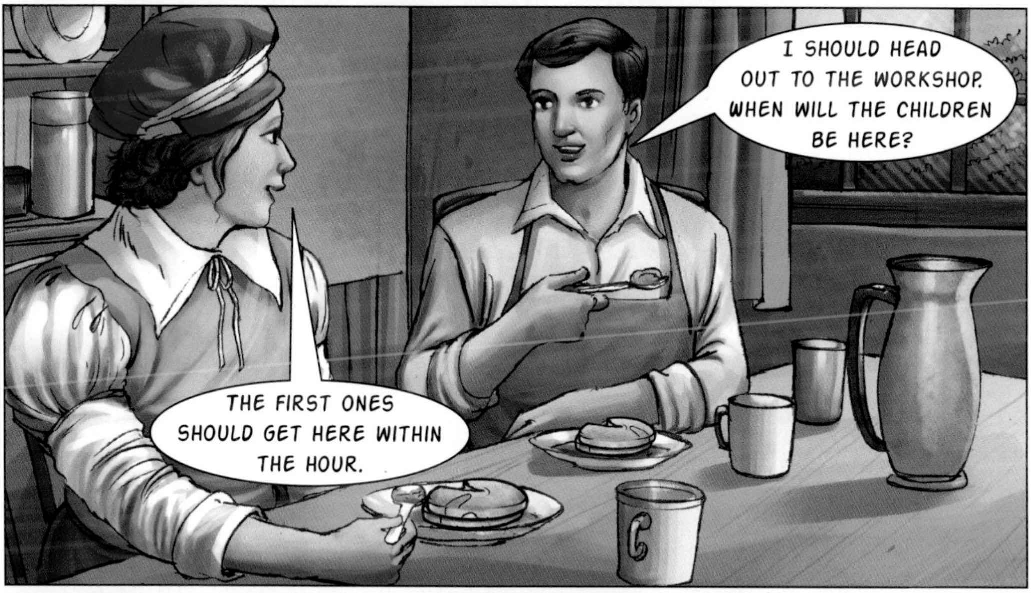
I SHOULD HEAD OUT TO THE WORKSHOP. WHEN WILL THE CHILDREN BE HERE?
THE FIRST ONES SHOULD GET HERE WITHIN THE HOUR.

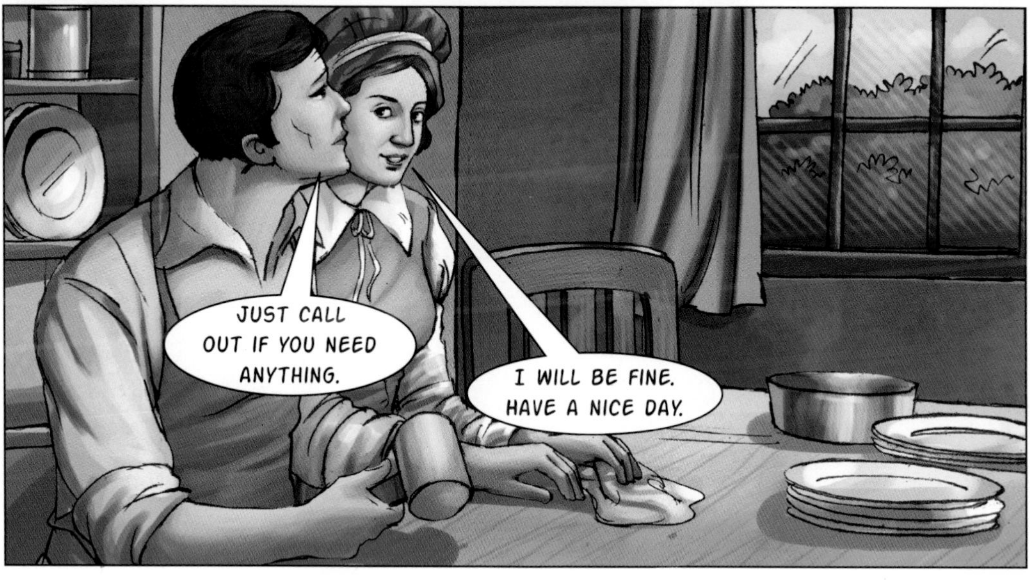
JUST CALL OUT IF YOU NEED ANYTHING.
I WILL BE FINE. HAVE A NICE DAY.

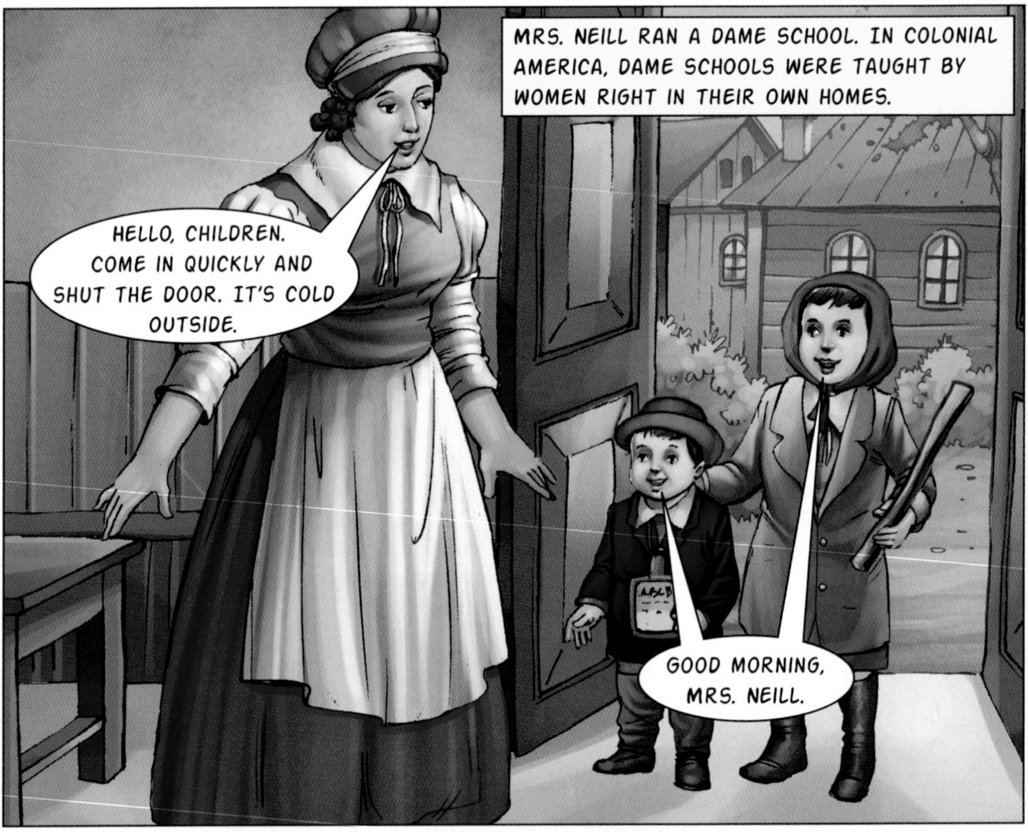
MRS. NEILL RAN A DAME SCHOOL. IN COLONIAL AMERICA, DAME SCHOOLS WERE TAUGHT BY WOMEN RIGHT IN THEIR OWN HOMES.
HELLO, CHILDREN. COME IN QUICKLY AND SHUT THE DOOR. IT'S COLD OUTSIDE.
GOOD MORNING, MRS. NEILL.

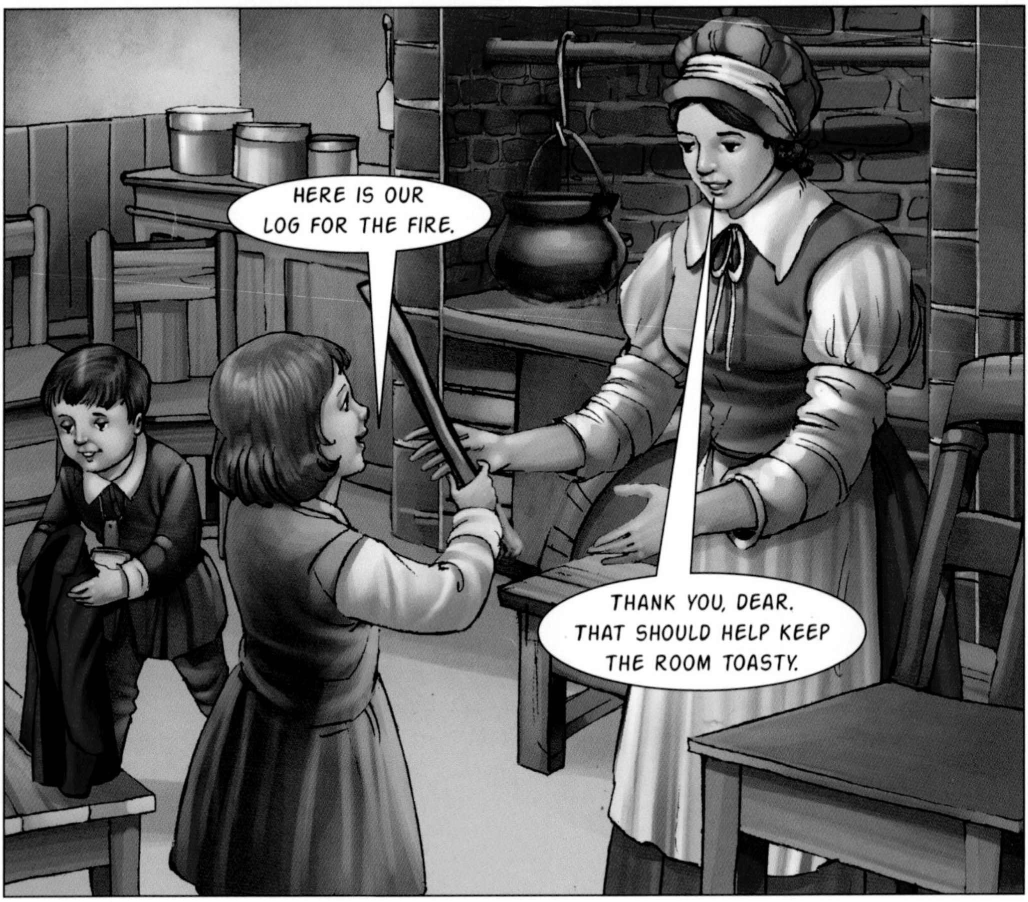
HERE IS OUR LOG FOR THE FIRE.
THANK YOU, DEAR. THAT SHOULD HELP KEEP THE ROOM TOASTY.

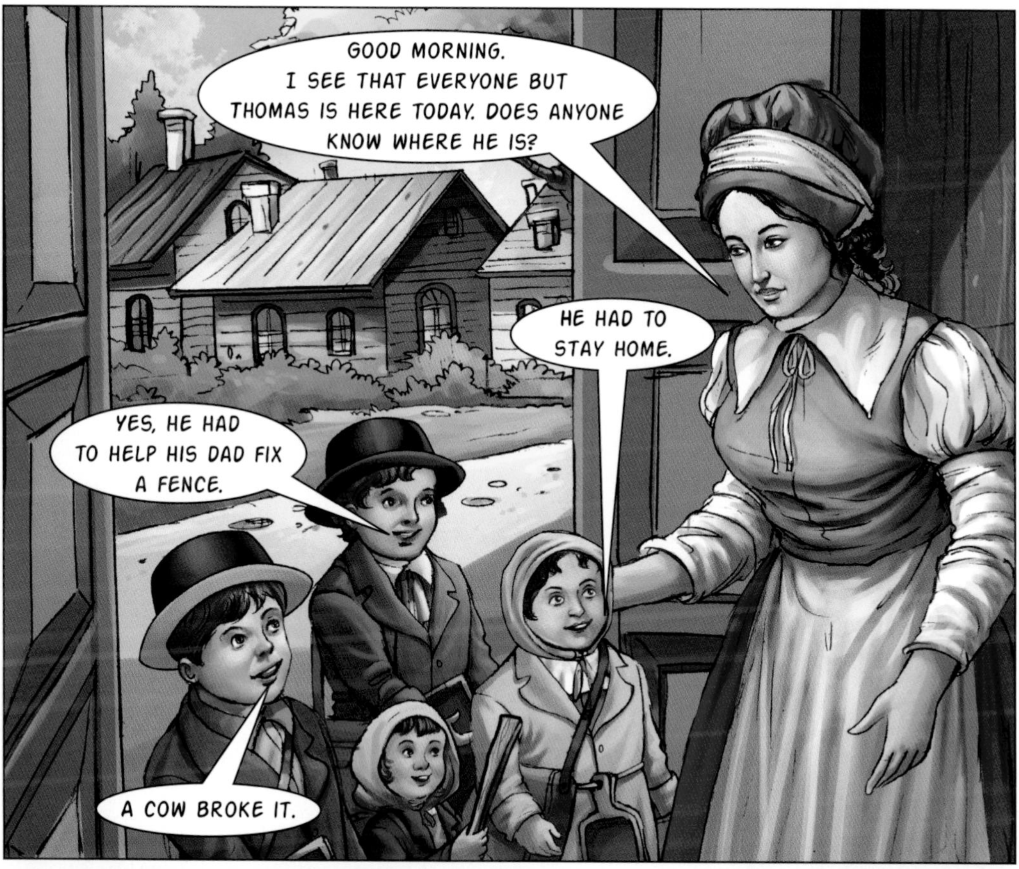
GOOD MORNING. I SEE THAT EVERYONE BUT THOMAS IS HERE TODAY. DOES ANYONE KNOW WHERE HE IS?
HE HAD TO STAY HOME.
YES, HE HAD TO HELP HIS DAD FIX A FENCE.
A COW BROKE IT.

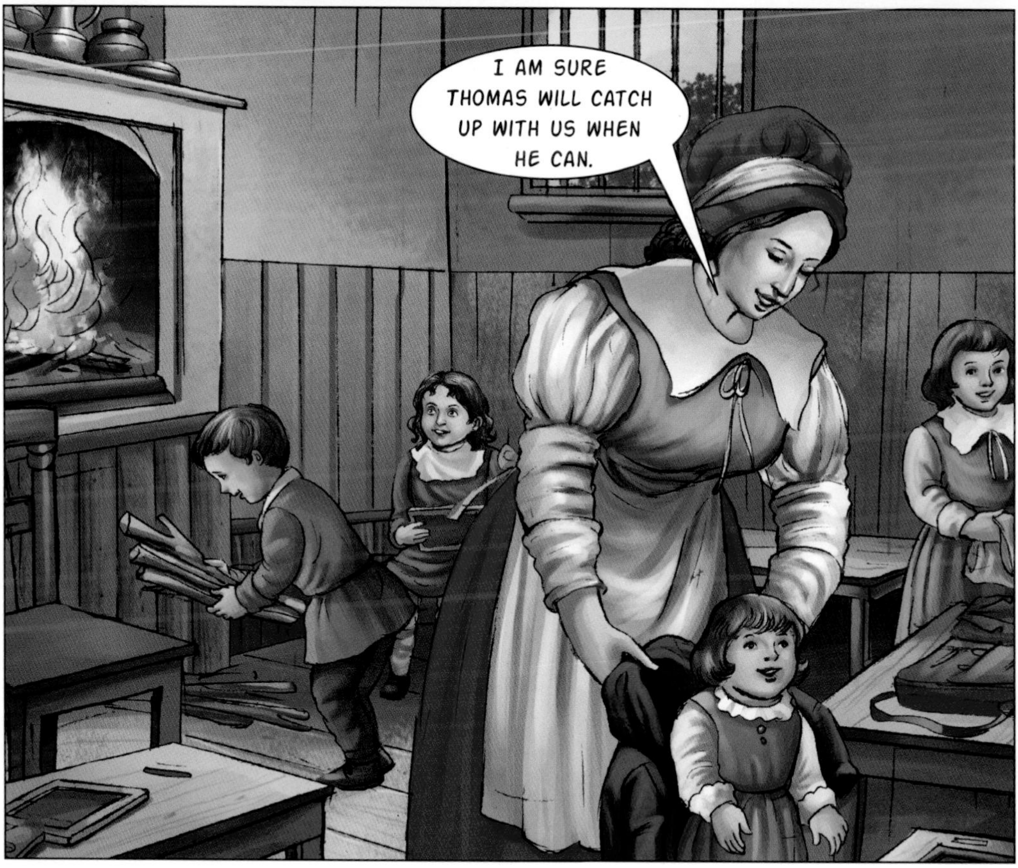
I AM SURE THOMAS WILL CATCH UP WITH US WHEN HE CAN.

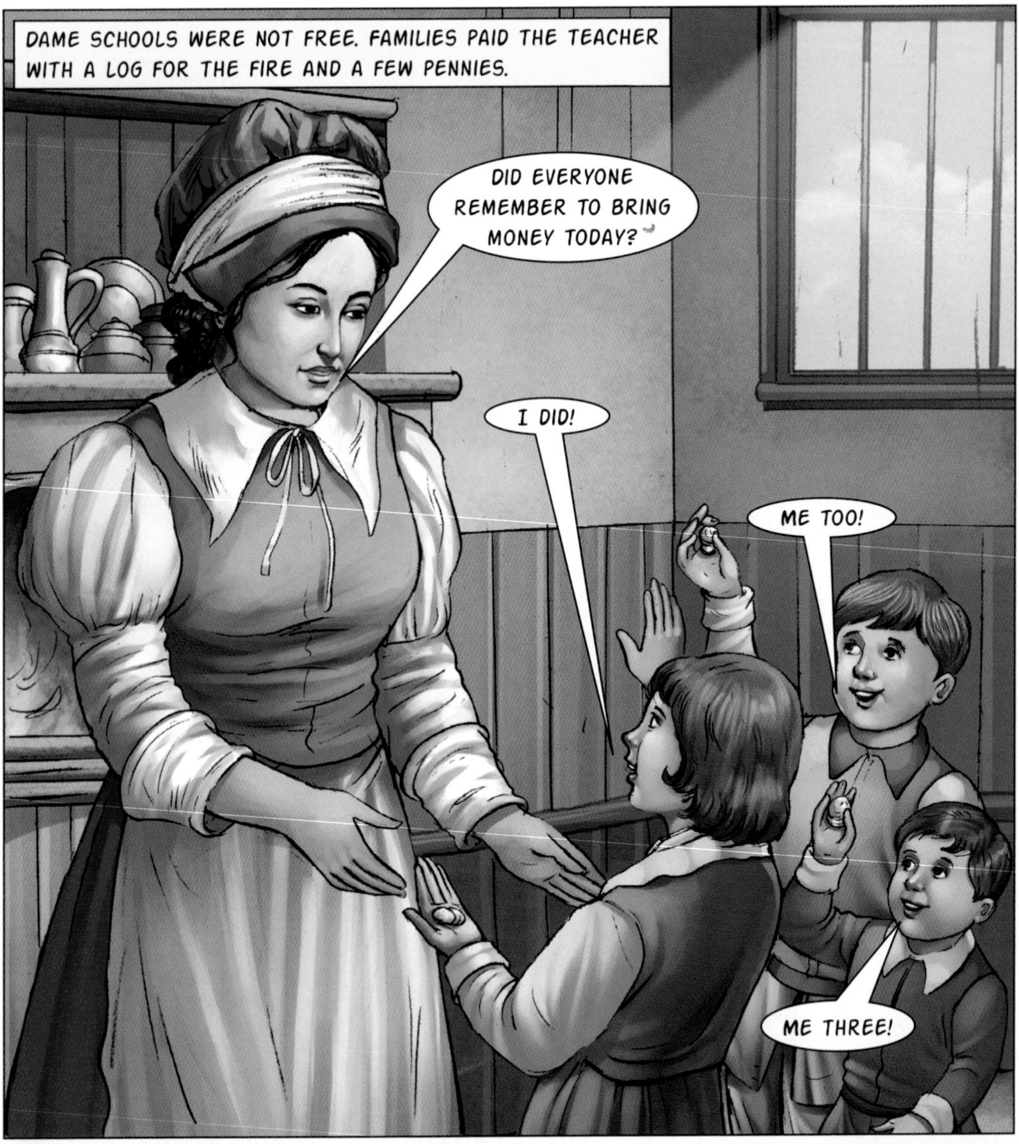
DAME SCHOOLS WERE NOT FREE. FAMILIES PAID THE TEACHER WITH A LOG FOR THE FIRE AND A FEW PENNIES.
DID EVERYONE REMEMBER TO BRING MONEY TODAY?
I DID!
ME TOO!
ME THREE!

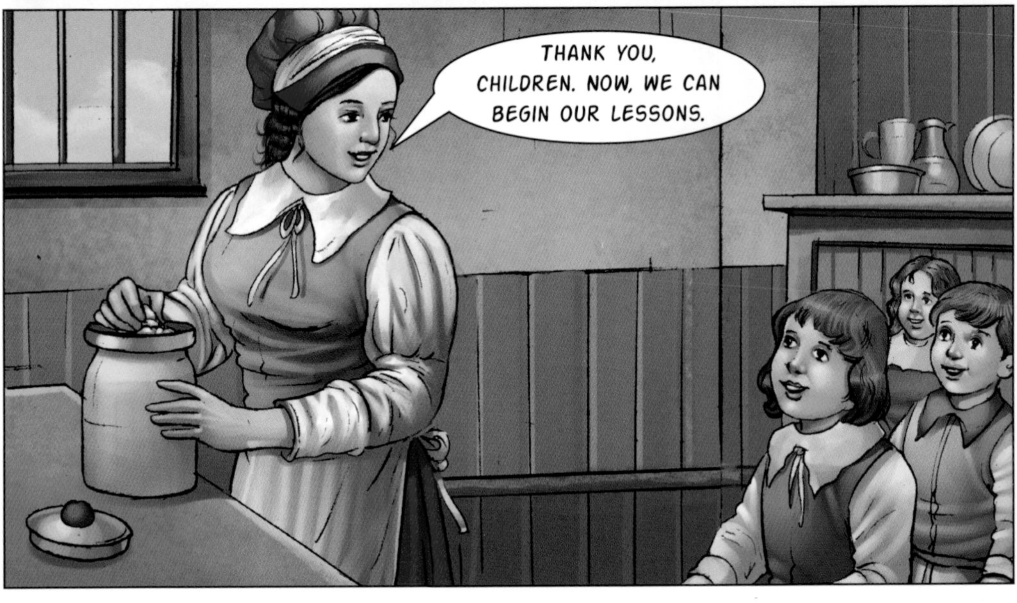
THANK YOU, CHILDREN. NOW, WE CAN BEGIN OUR LESSONS.

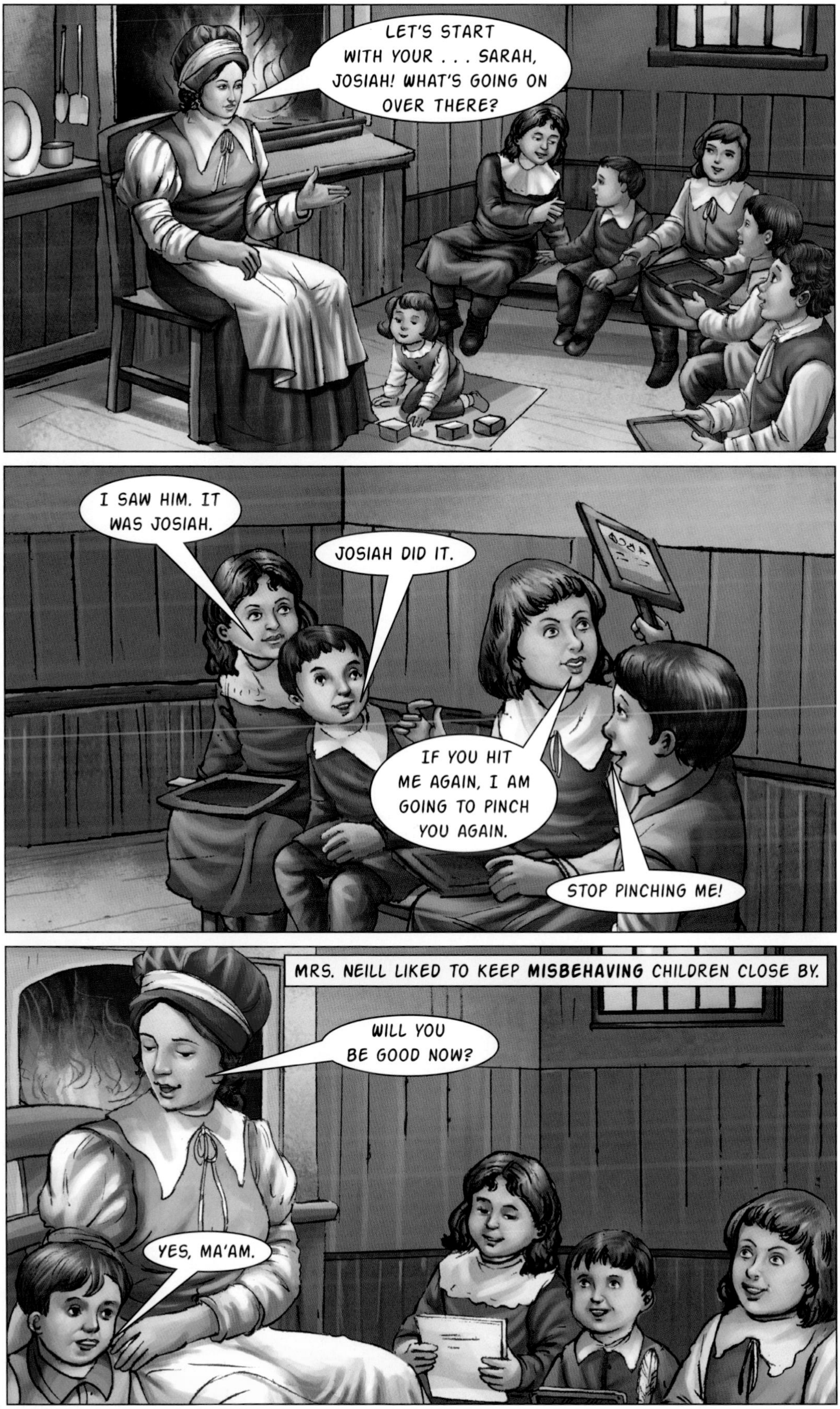
LET'S START WITH YOUR . . . SARAH, JOSIAH! WHAT'S GOING ON OVER THERE?
I SAW HIM. IT WAS JOSIAH.
JOSIAH DID IT.
IF YOU HIT ME AGAIN, I AM GOING TO PINCH YOU AGAIN.
STOP PINCHING ME!
MRS. NEILL LIKED TO KEEP MISBEHAVING CHILDREN CLOSE BY.
WILL YOU BE GOOD NOW?
YES, MA'AM.

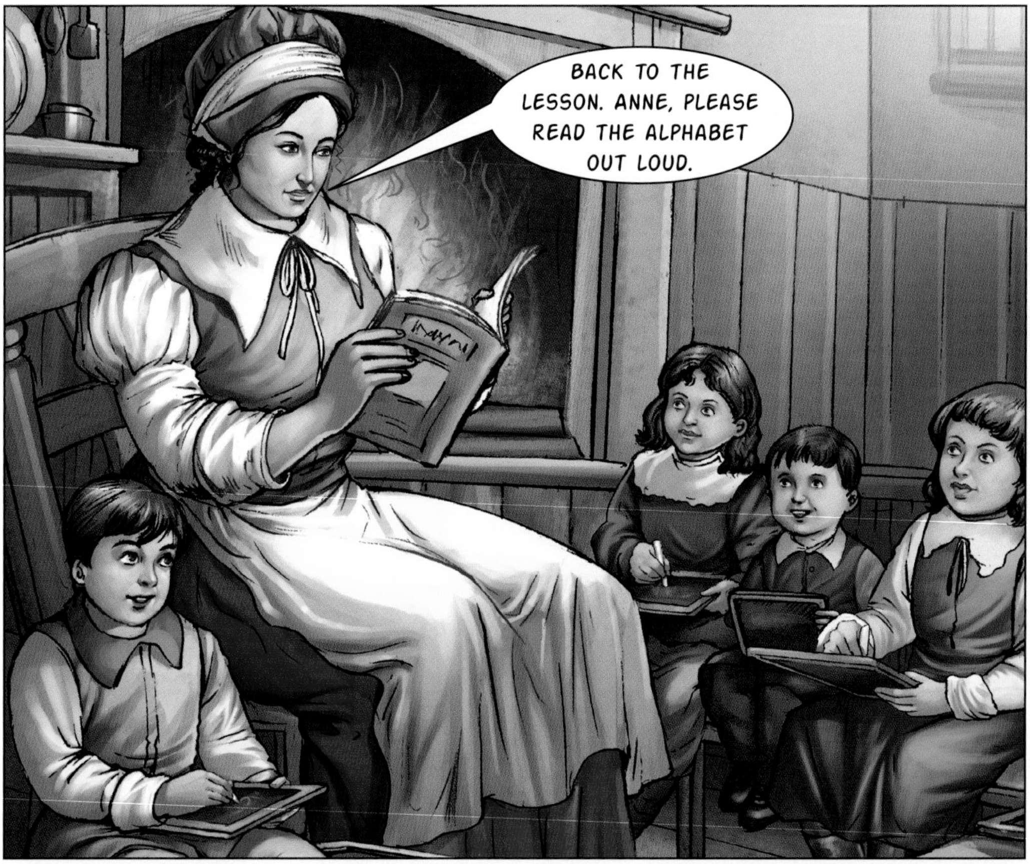
BACK TO THE LESSON. ANNE, PLEASE READ THE ALPHABET OUT LOUD.

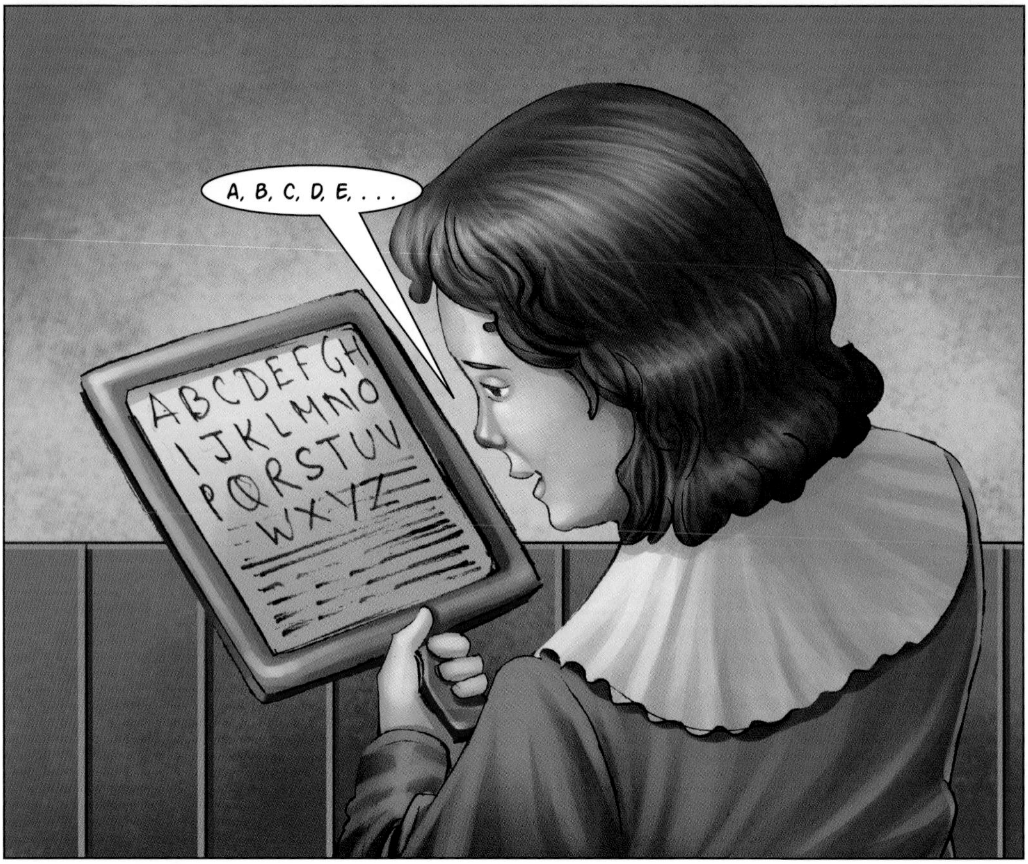
A, B, C, D, E, . . .

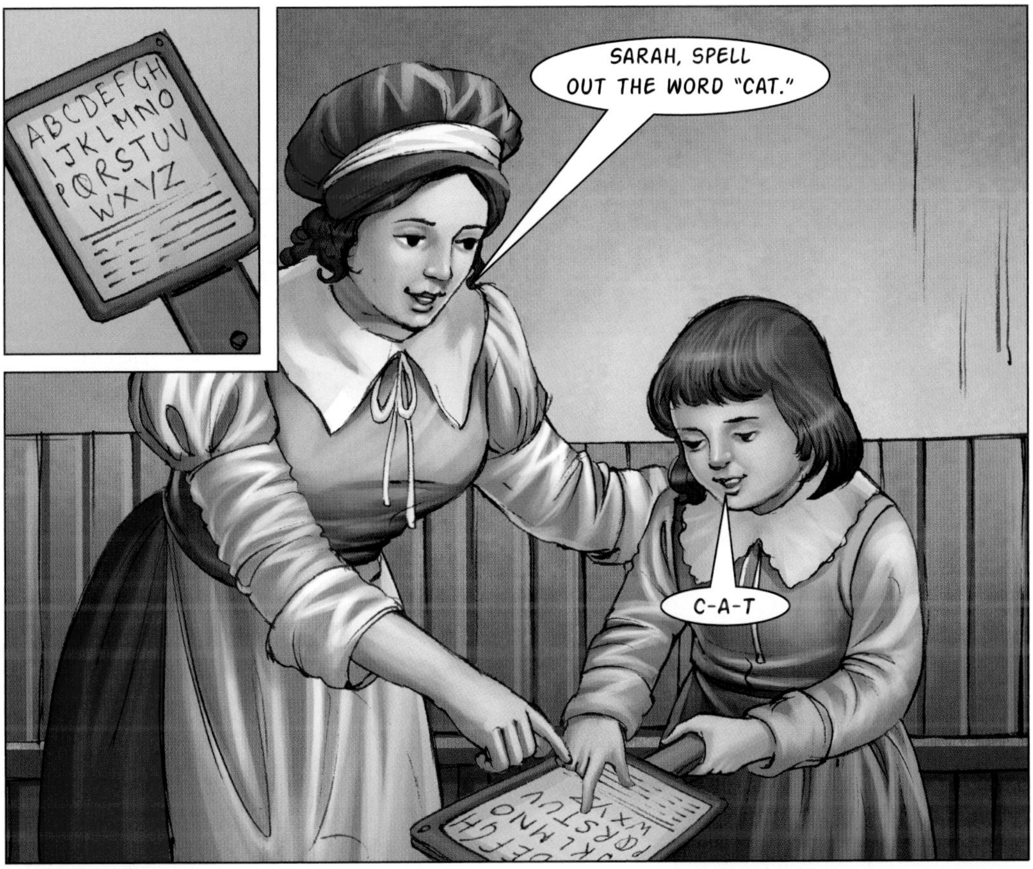
ABCDEFGH
IJKLMNO
PQRSTUV
WXYZ
SARAH, SPELL OUT THE WORD "CAT."
C-A-T

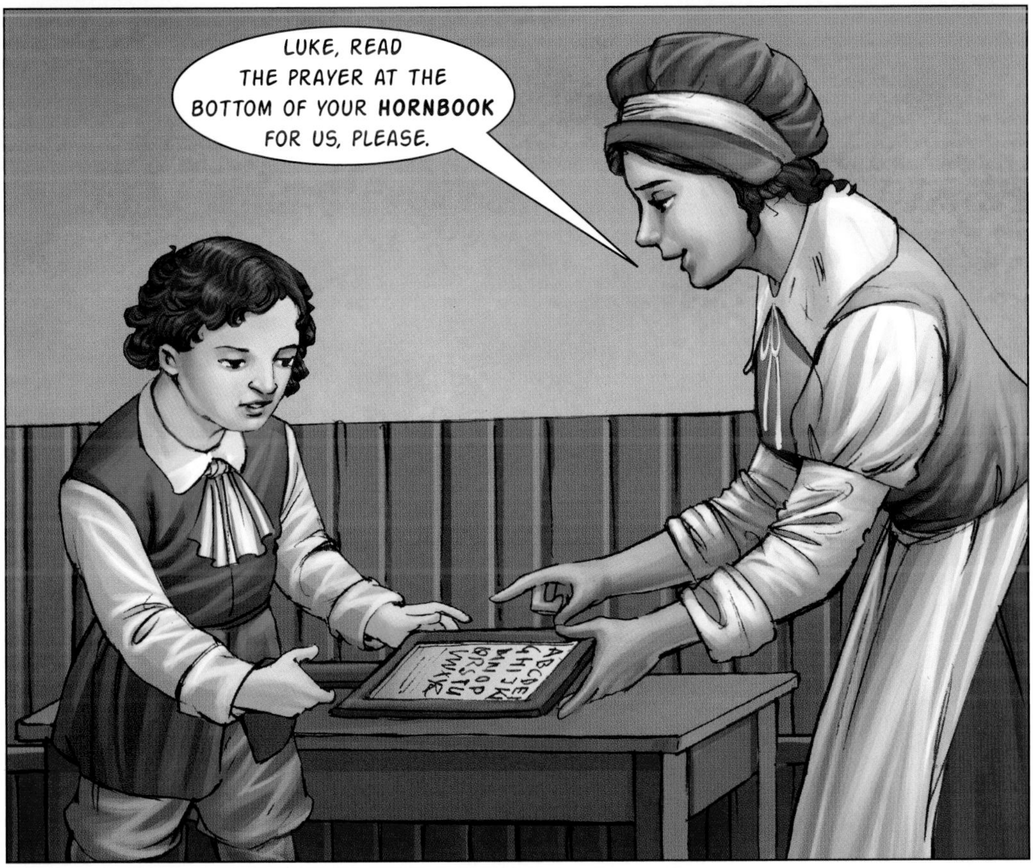
LUKE, READ THE PRAYER AT THE BOTTOM OF YOUR **HORNBOOK** FOR US, PLEASE.

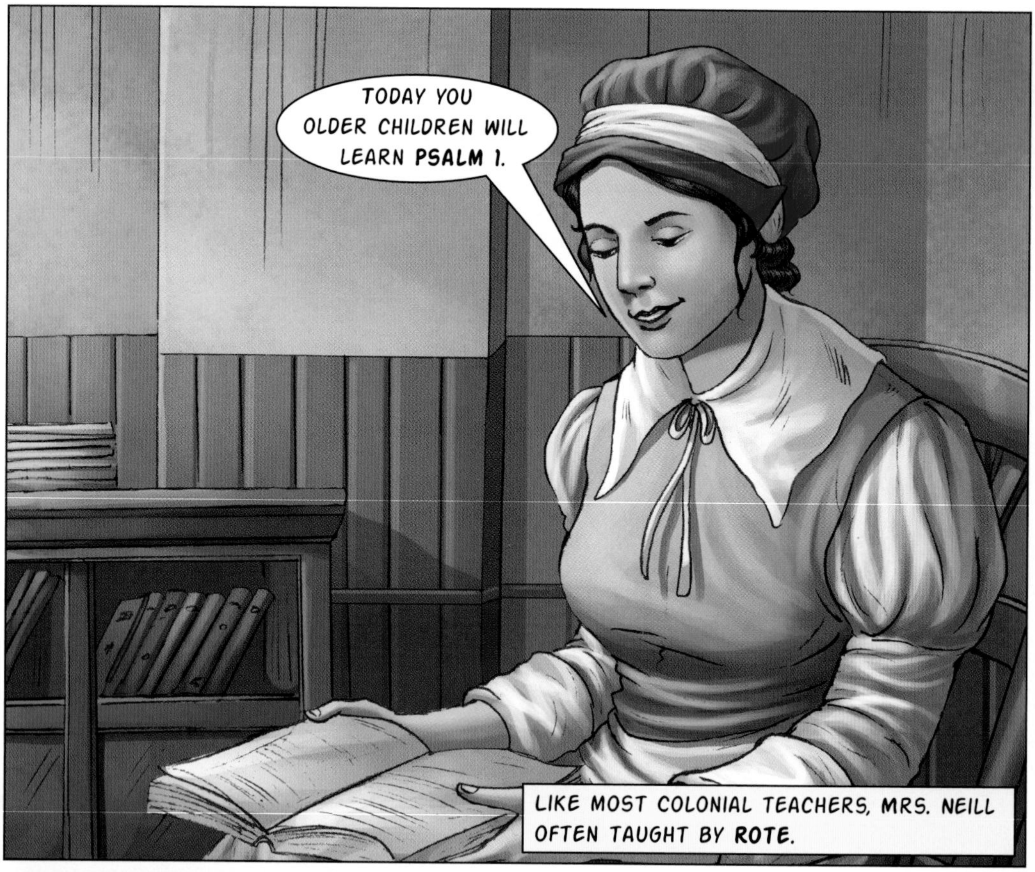
TODAY YOU OLDER CHILDREN WILL LEARN **PSALM 1**.
LIKE MOST COLONIAL TEACHERS, MRS. NEILL OFTEN TAUGHT BY **ROTE**.

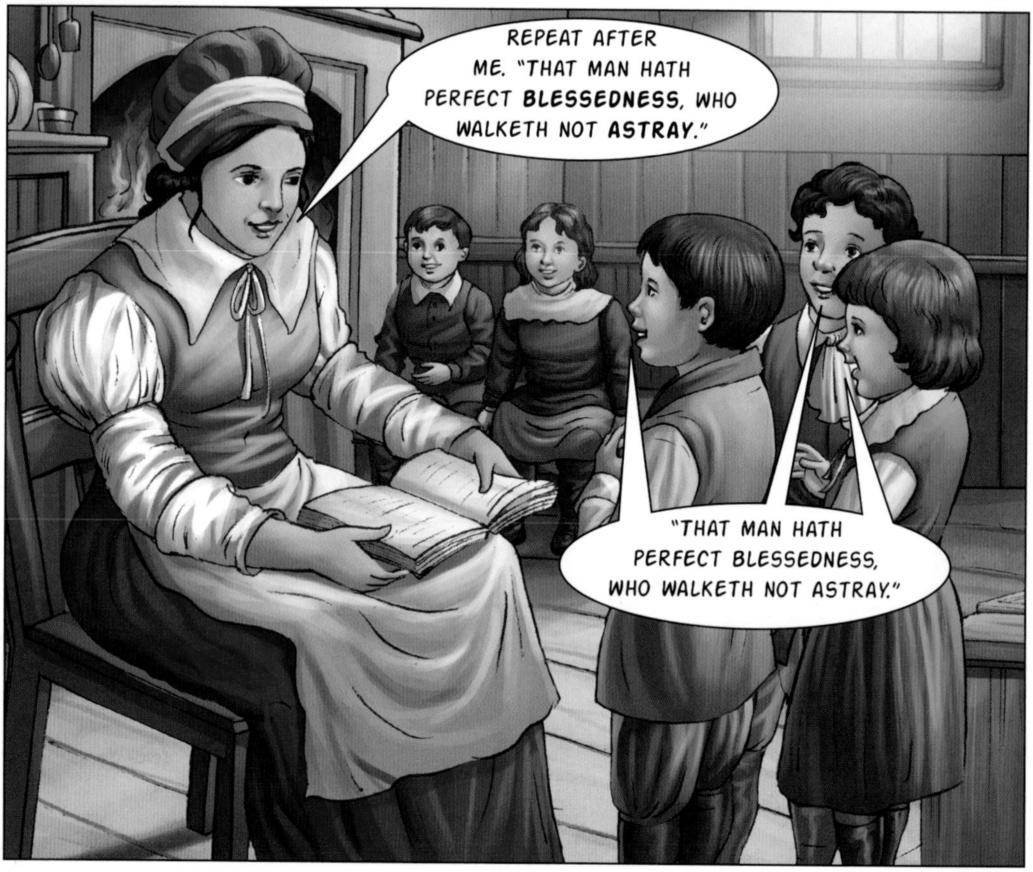
REPEAT AFTER ME. "THAT MAN HATH PERFECT **BLESSEDNESS**, WHO WALKETH NOT **ASTRAY**."
"THAT MAN HATH PERFECT BLESSEDNESS, WHO WALKETH NOT ASTRAY."

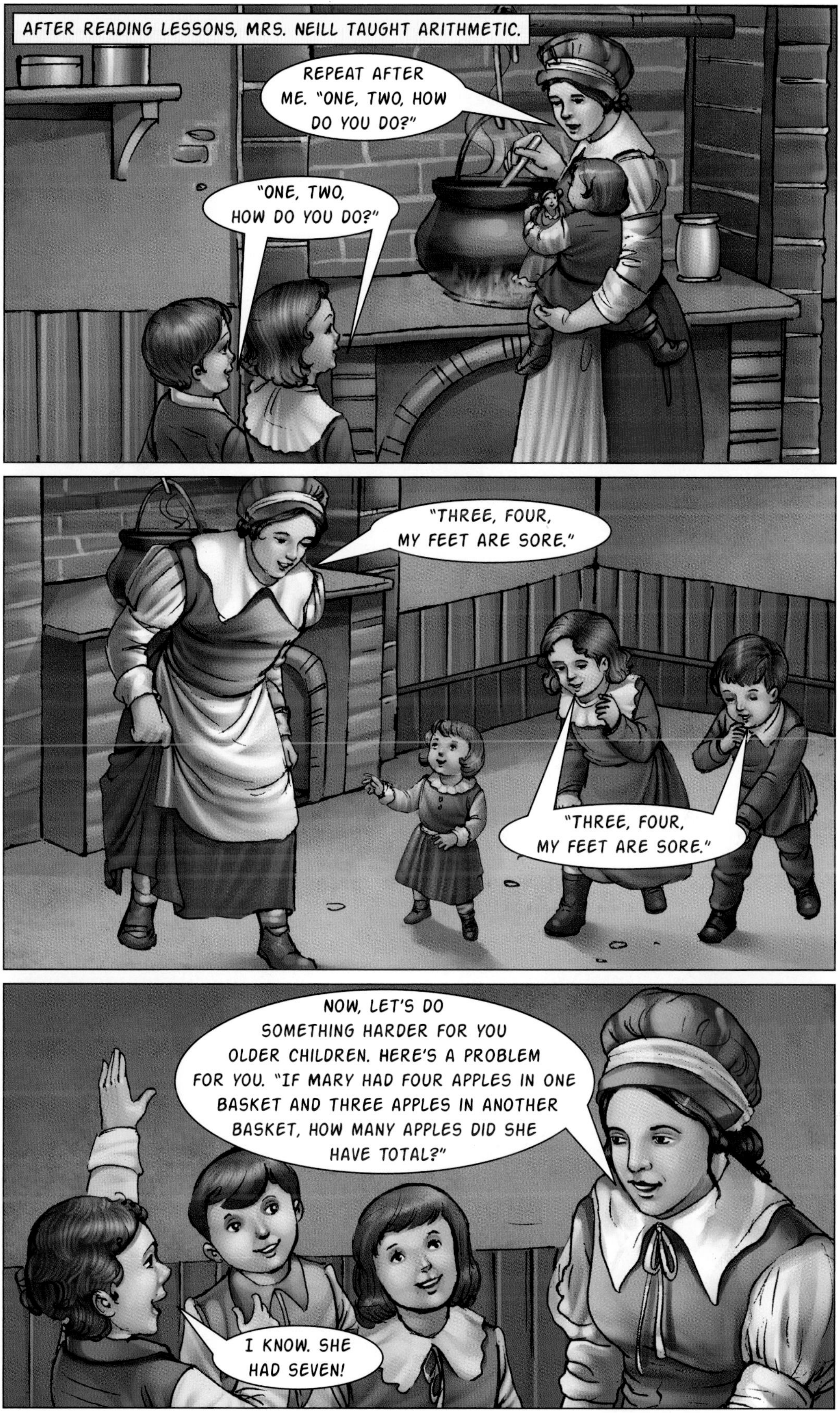
AFTER READING LESSONS, MRS. NEILL TAUGHT ARITHMETIC.
REPEAT AFTER ME. "ONE, TWO, HOW DO YOU DO?"
"ONE, TWO, HOW DO YOU DO?"
"THREE, FOUR, MY FEET ARE SORE."
"THREE, FOUR, MY FEET ARE SORE."
NOW, LET'S DO SOMETHING HARDER FOR YOU OLDER CHILDREN. HERE'S A PROBLEM FOR YOU. "IF MARY HAD FOUR APPLES IN ONE BASKET AND THREE APPLES IN ANOTHER BASKET, HOW MANY APPLES DID SHE HAVE TOTAL?"
I KNOW. SHE HAD SEVEN!

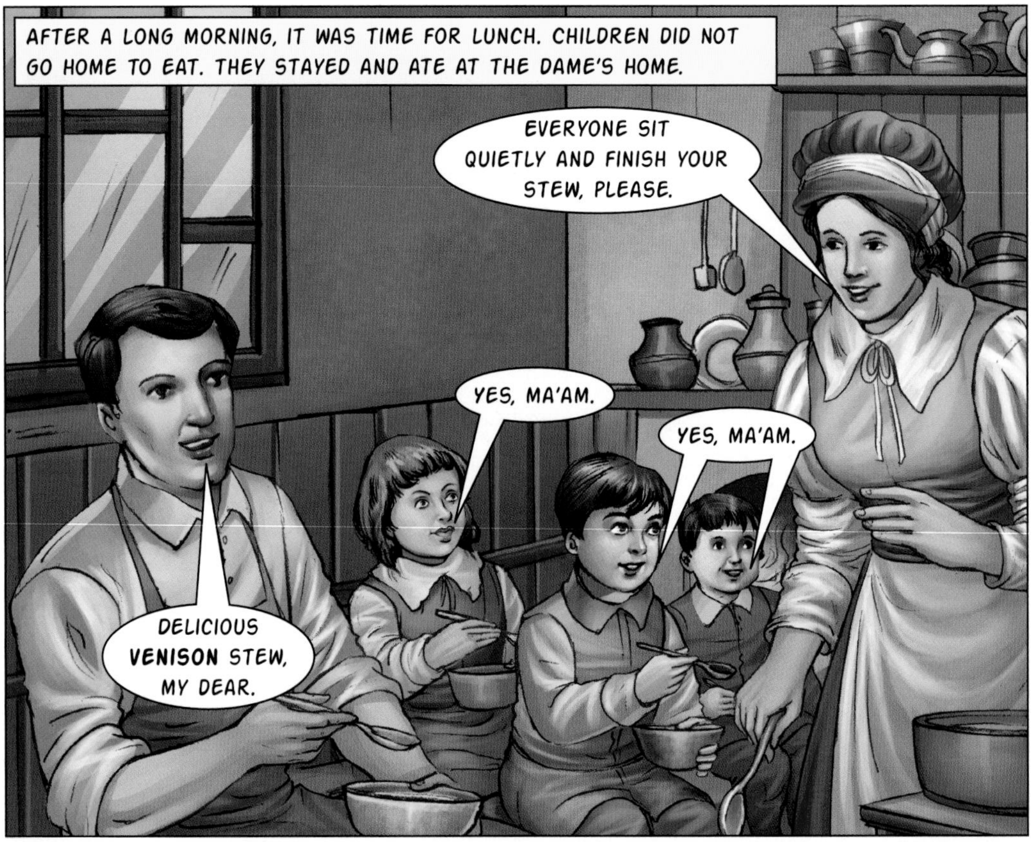
AFTER A LONG MORNING, IT WAS TIME FOR LUNCH. CHILDREN DID NOT GO HOME TO EAT. THEY STAYED AND ATE AT THE DAME'S HOME.
EVERYONE SIT QUIETLY AND FINISH YOUR STEW, PLEASE.
DELICIOUS **VENISON** STEW, MY DEAR.
YES, MA'AM.
YES, MA'AM.

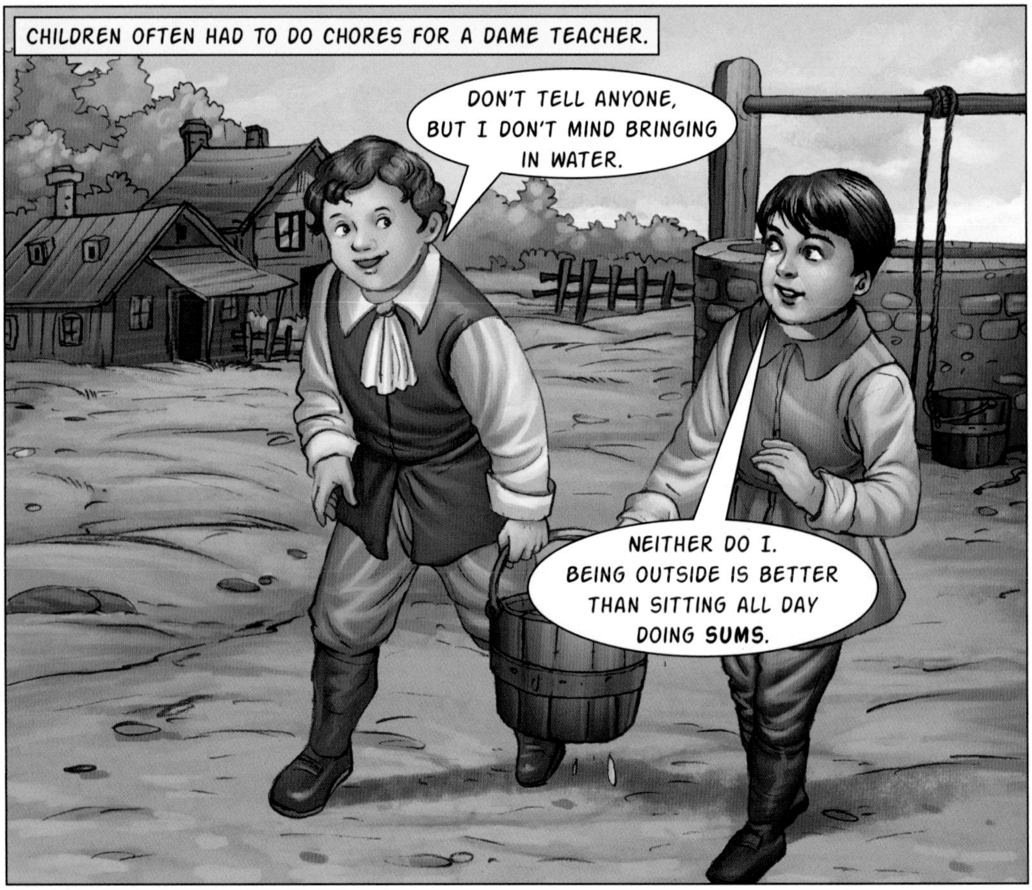
CHILDREN OFTEN HAD TO DO CHORES FOR A DAME TEACHER.
DON'T TELL ANYONE, BUT I DON'T MIND BRINGING IN WATER.
NEITHER DO I. BEING OUTSIDE IS BETTER THAN SITTING ALL DAY DOING **SUMS**.

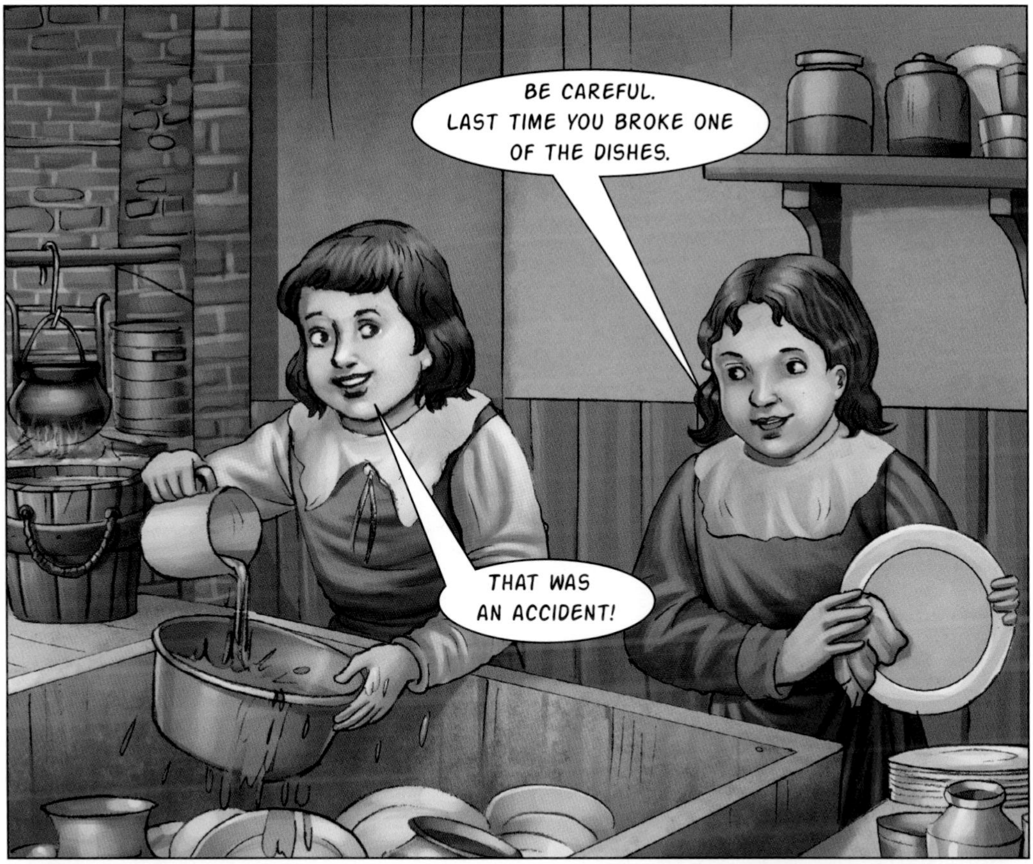
BE CAREFUL.
LAST TIME YOU BROKE ONE OF THE DISHES.
THAT WAS AN ACCIDENT!

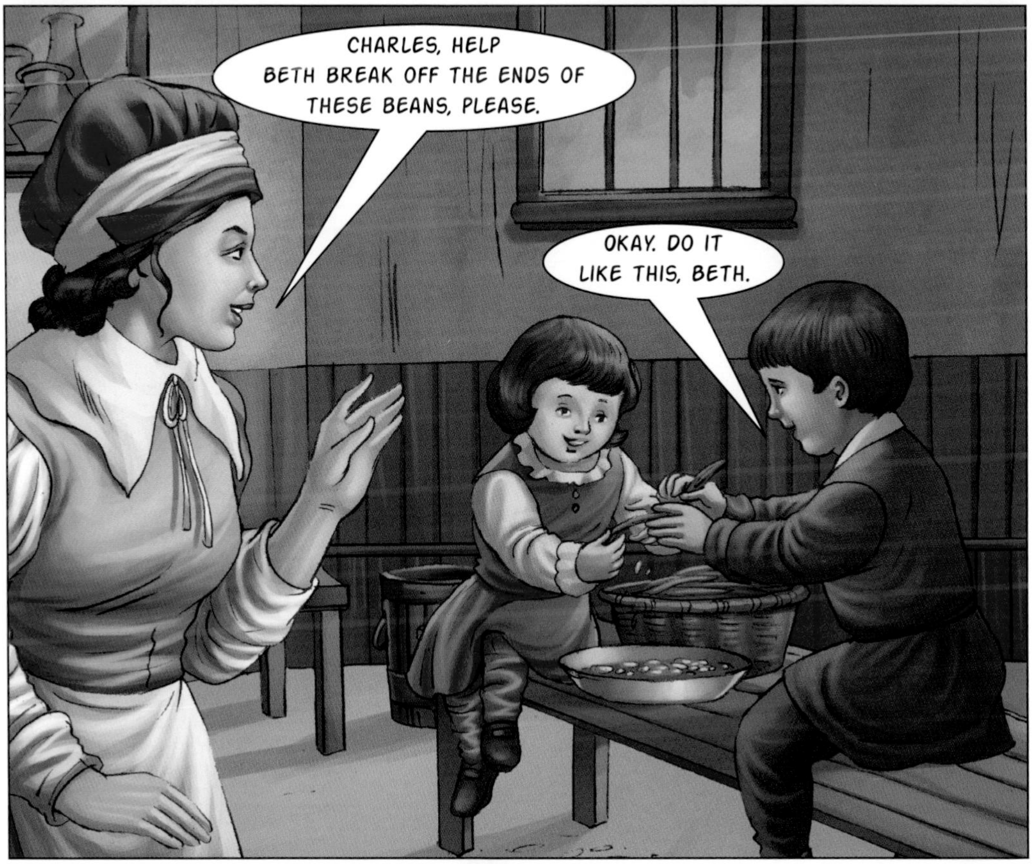
CHARLES, HELP BETH BREAK OFF THE ENDS OF THESE BEANS, PLEASE.
OKAY. DO IT LIKE THIS, BETH.

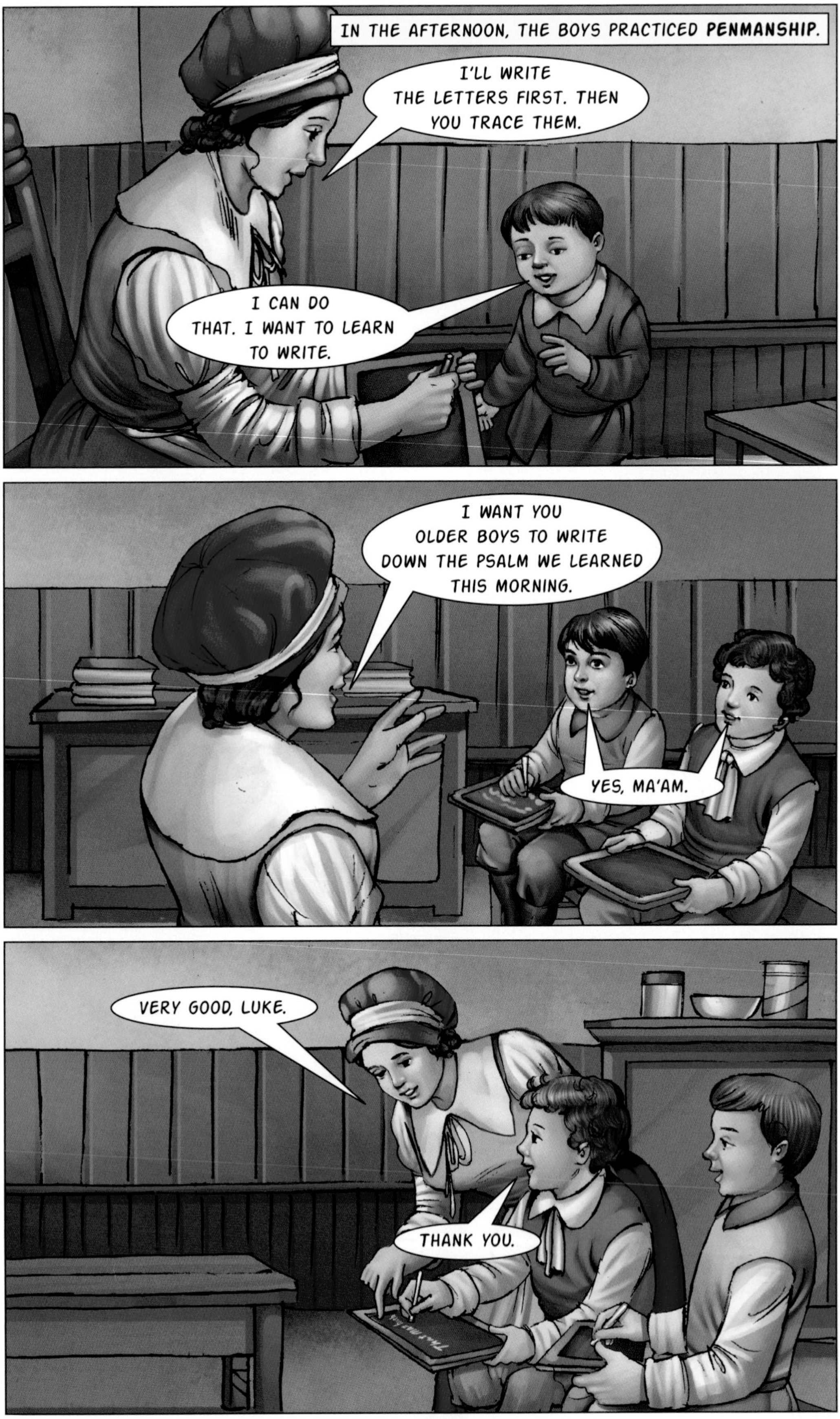
IN THE AFTERNOON, THE BOYS PRACTICED **PENMANSHIP**.
I'LL WRITE THE LETTERS FIRST. THEN YOU TRACE THEM.
I CAN DO THAT. I WANT TO LEARN TO WRITE.
I WANT YOU OLDER BOYS TO WRITE DOWN THE PSALM WE LEARNED THIS MORNING.
YES, MA'AM.
VERY GOOD, LUKE.
THANK YOU.

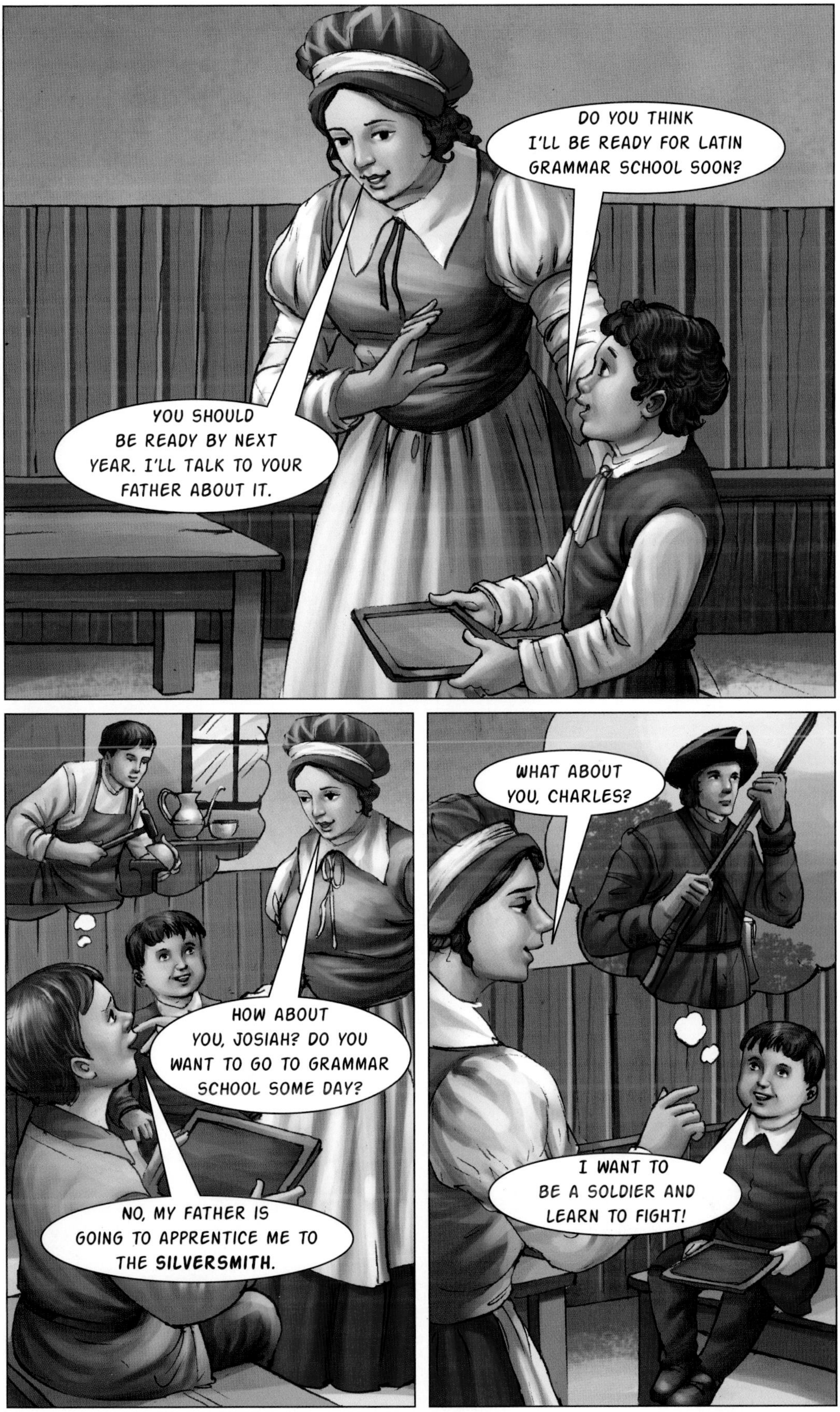
DO YOU THINK I'LL BE READY FOR LATIN GRAMMAR SCHOOL SOON?
YOU SHOULD BE READY BY NEXT YEAR. I'LL TALK TO YOUR FATHER ABOUT IT.
HOW ABOUT YOU, JOSIAH? DO YOU WANT TO GO TO GRAMMAR SCHOOL SOME DAY?
NO, MY FATHER IS GOING TO APPRENTICE ME TO THE **SILVERSMITH**.
WHAT ABOUT YOU, CHARLES?
I WANT TO BE A SOLDIER AND LEARN TO FIGHT!

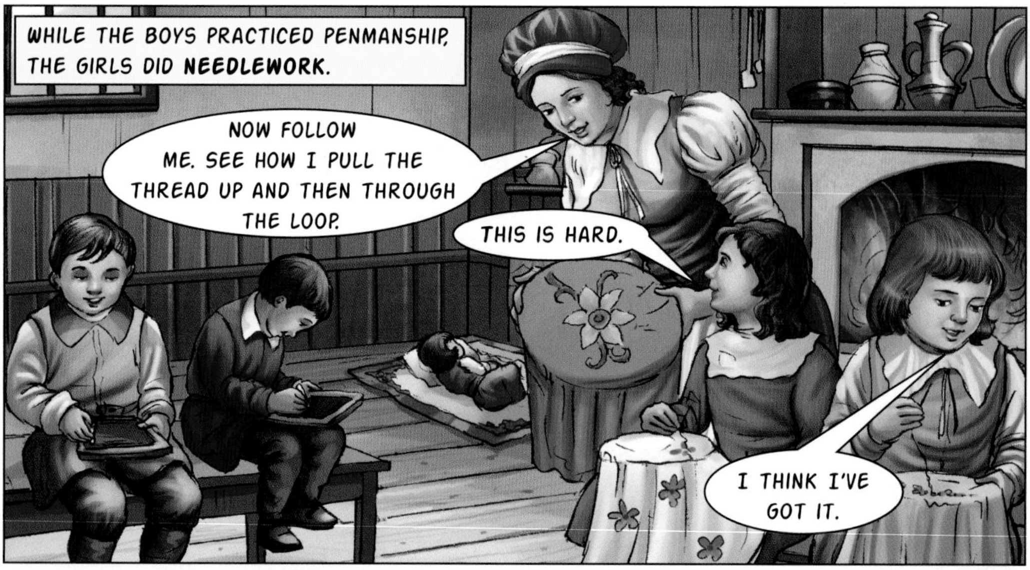
WHILE THE BOYS PRACTICED PENMANSHIP, THE GIRLS DID **NEEDLEWORK**.
NOW FOLLOW ME. SEE HOW I PULL THE THREAD UP AND THEN THROUGH THE LOOP.
THIS IS HARD.
I THINK I'VE GOT IT.

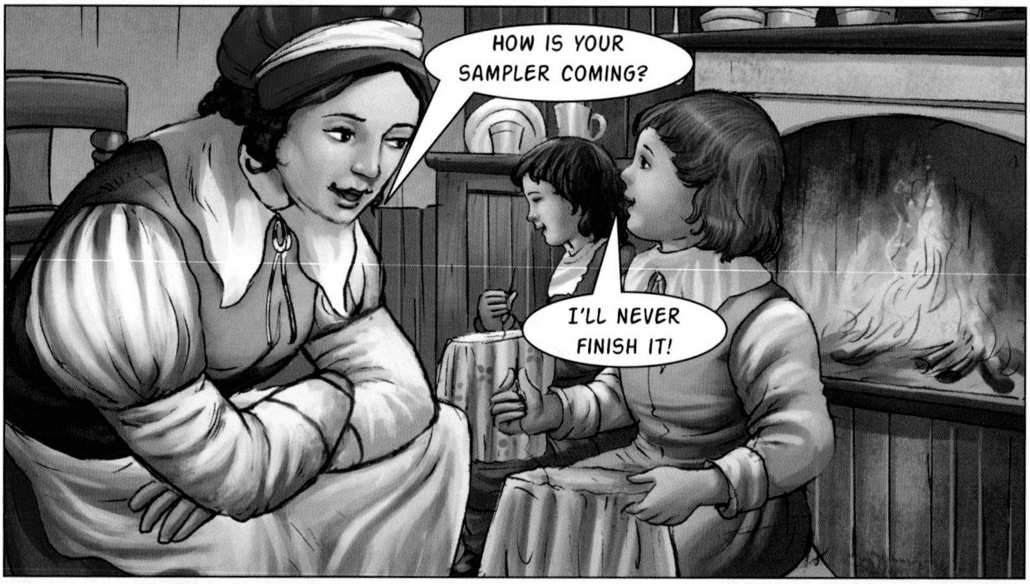
HOW IS YOUR SAMPLER COMING?
I'LL NEVER FINISH IT!

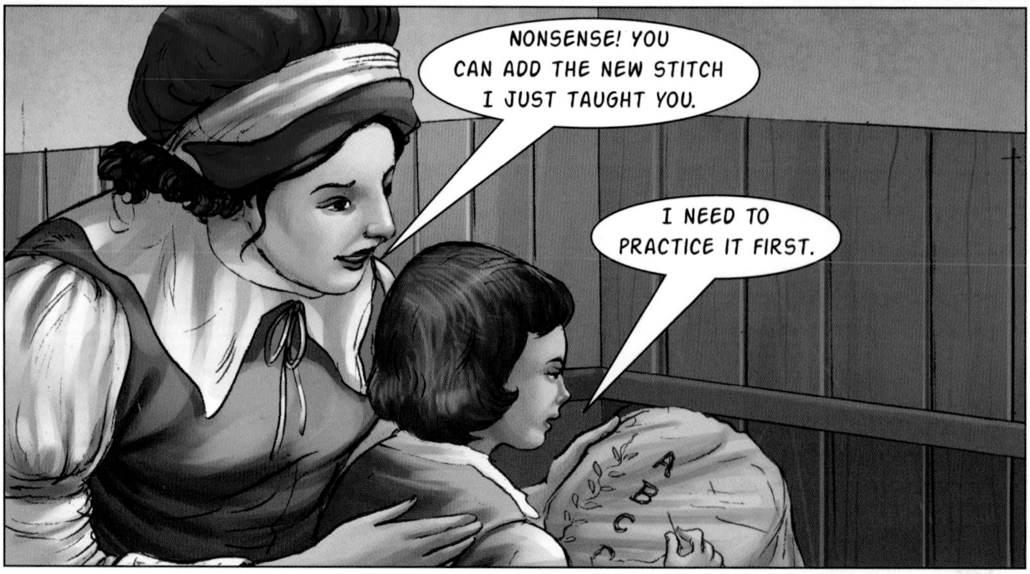
NONSENSE! YOU CAN ADD THE NEW STITCH I JUST TAUGHT YOU.
I NEED TO PRACTICE IT FIRST.

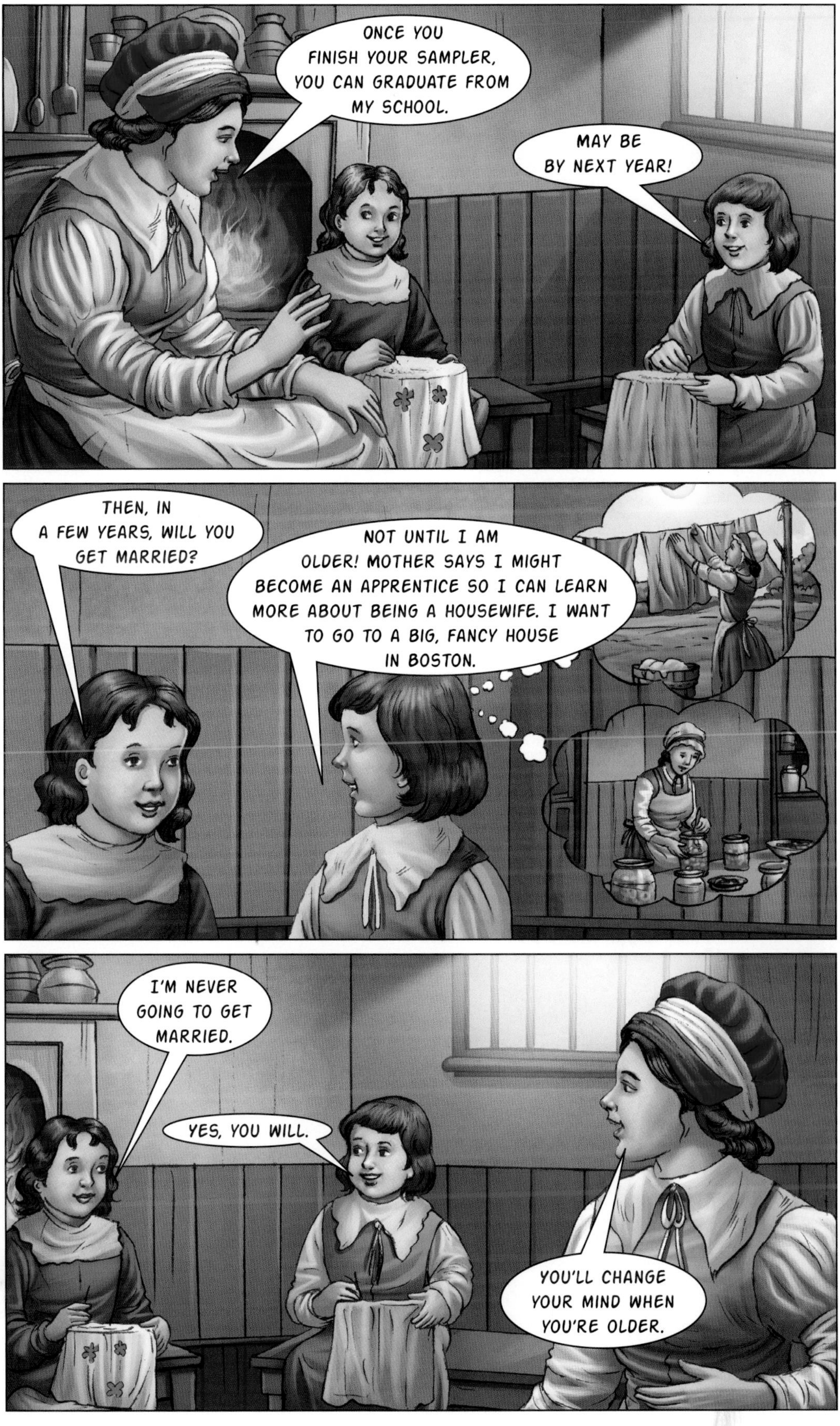
ONCE YOU FINISH YOUR SAMPLER, YOU CAN GRADUATE FROM MY SCHOOL.
MAY BE BY NEXT YEAR!
THEN, IN A FEW YEARS, WILL YOU GET MARRIED?
NOT UNTIL I AM OLDER! MOTHER SAYS I MIGHT BECOME AN APPRENTICE SO I CAN LEARN MORE ABOUT BEING A HOUSEWIFE. I WANT TO GO TO A BIG, FANCY HOUSE IN BOSTON.
I'M NEVER GOING TO GET MARRIED.
YES, YOU WILL.
YOU'LL CHANGE YOUR MIND WHEN YOU'RE OLDER.

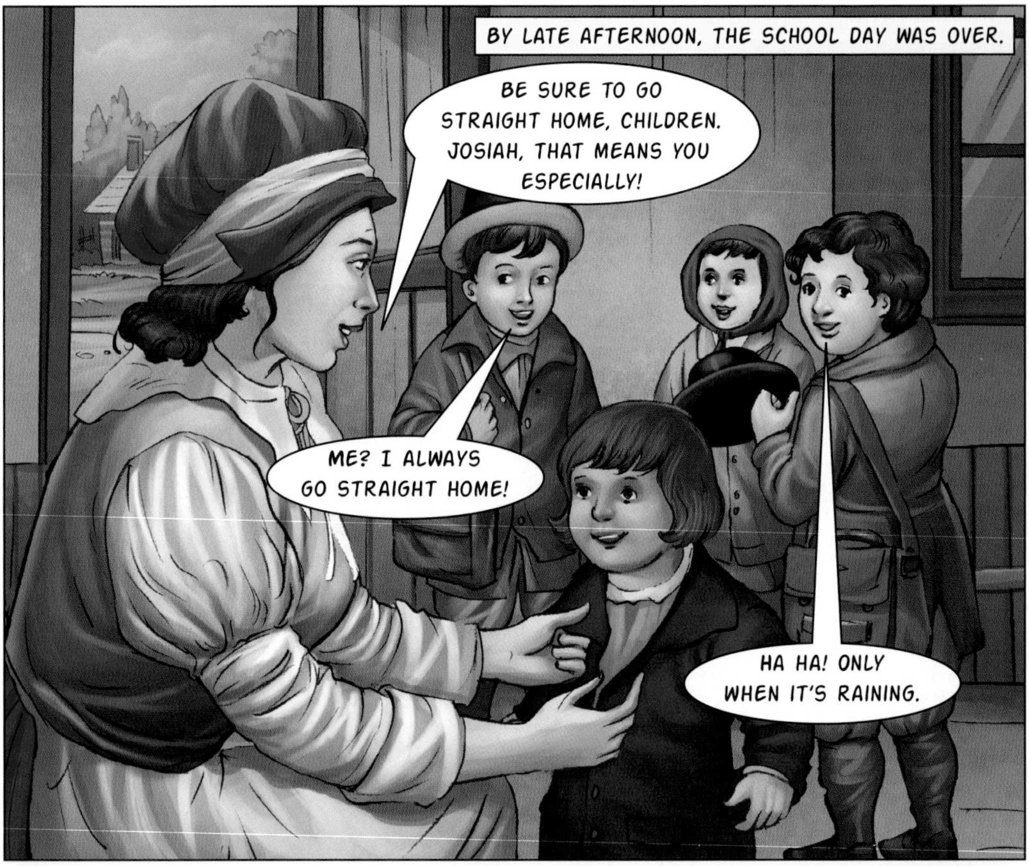
BY LATE AFTERNOON, THE SCHOOL DAY WAS OVER.
BE SURE TO GO STRAIGHT HOME, CHILDREN. JOSIAH, THAT MEANS YOU ESPECIALLY!
ME? I ALWAYS GO STRAIGHT HOME!
HA HA! ONLY WHEN IT'S RAINING.

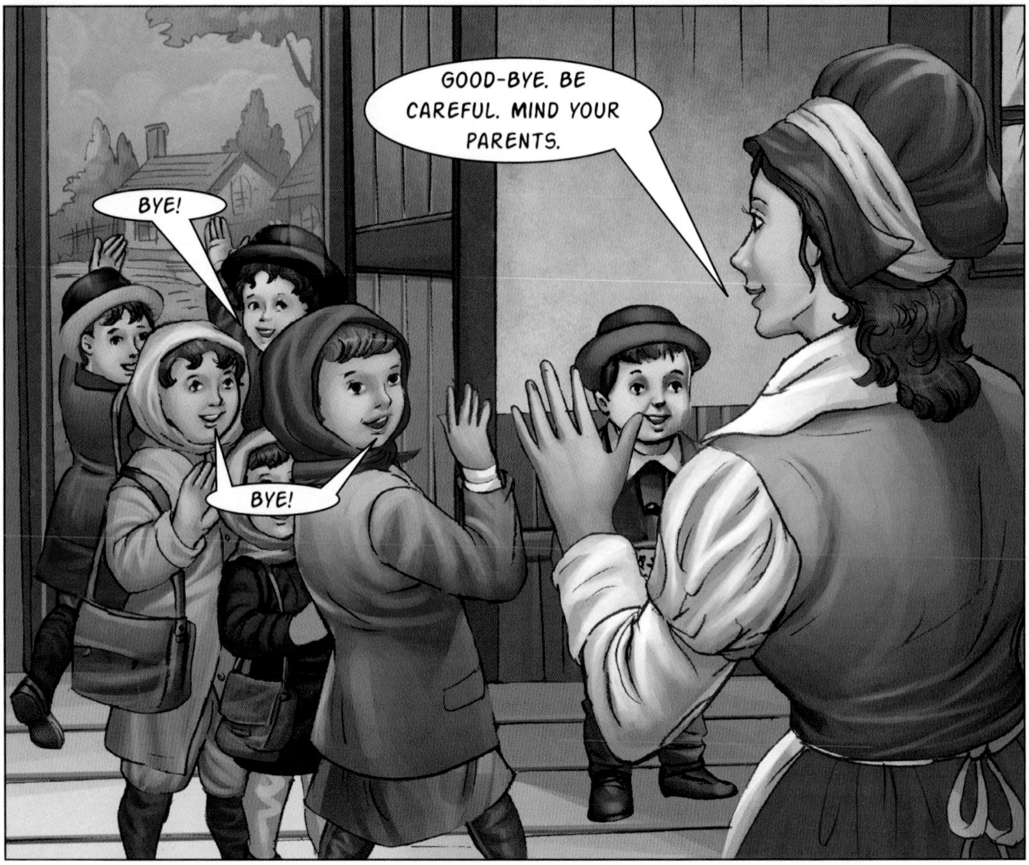
GOOD-BYE. BE CAREFUL. MIND YOUR PARENTS.
BYE!
BYE!

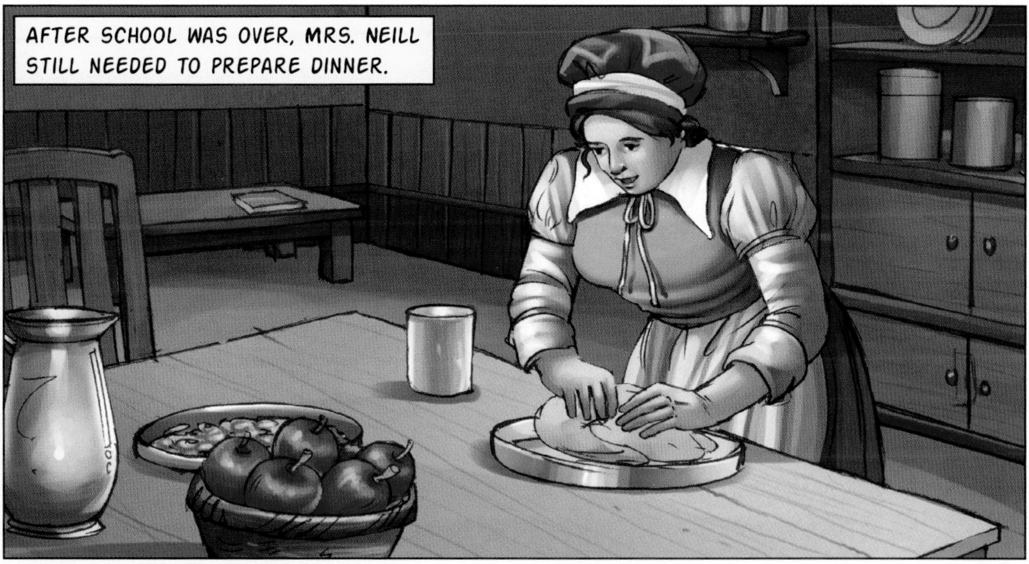
AFTER SCHOOL WAS OVER, MRS. NEILL STILL NEEDED TO PREPARE DINNER.

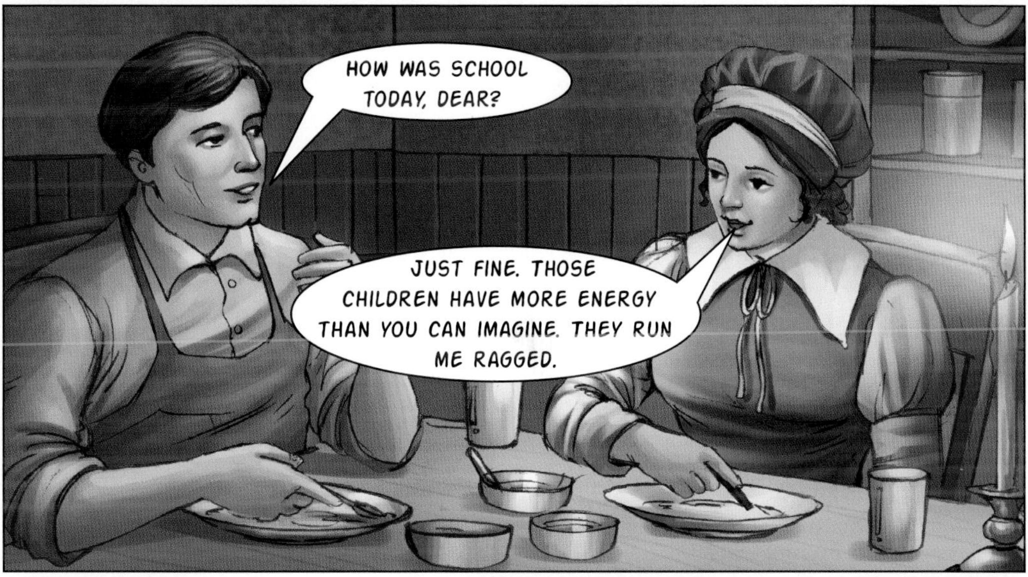
HOW WAS SCHOOL TODAY, DEAR?
JUST FINE. THOSE CHILDREN HAVE MORE ENERGY THAN YOU CAN IMAGINE. THEY RUN ME RAGGED.

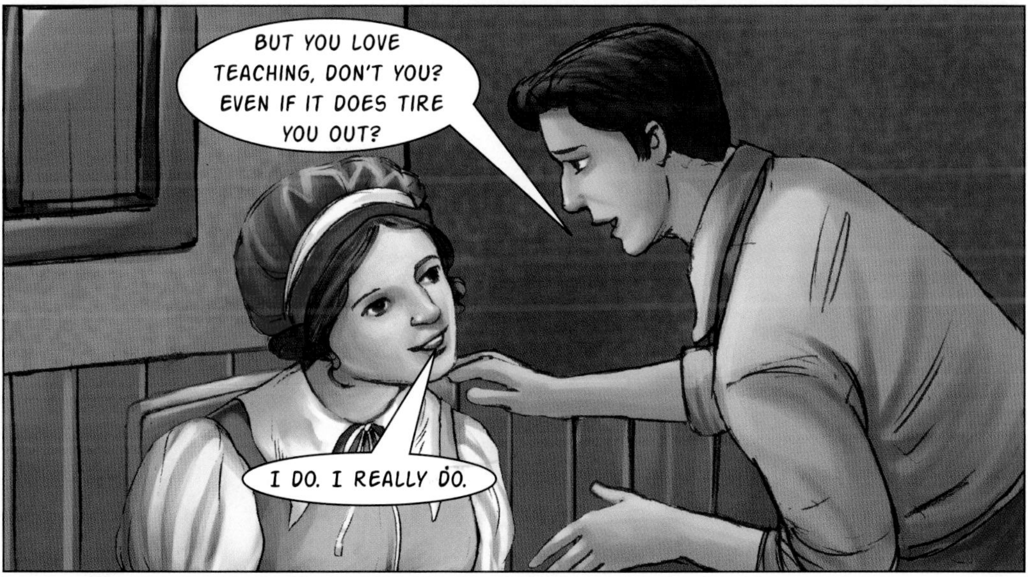
BUT YOU LOVE TEACHING, DON'T YOU? EVEN IF IT DOES TIRE YOU OUT?
I DO. I REALLY DO.

Famous Colonial Schoolteachers

Ezekiel Cheever
(1615–1708)

Ezekiel Cheever moved from Britain to America in 1637 and took a job as the master of a public school in New Haven, Connecticut. He taught in several schools throughout Connecticut before he took over as headmaster of the famous Boston Latin School, which prepared boys for attending university. Under Cheever, Boston Latin School became one of the finest schools in the country. Cheever also wrote a Latin textbook that became the standard text used in other Latin schools throughout New England.

James Maury
(1719–1769)

James Maury's parents moved the family from Ireland to America when Maury was just a baby. Eventually, he became a minister and ran the Albemarle Parish in Virginia from 1751 until he died in 1769. Like many ministers of the time, he became a teacher for an additional salary. He opened the Maury School for Boys and covered subjects that included the classics, manners and morals, mathematics, and geography. Three of Maury's students were future presidents of the United States: Thomas Jefferson, James Madison, and James Monroe.

Ann Wager
(1716–1774)

After Ann Wager's husband died in 1748, Wager began tutoring children to support herself and her family. By the early 1760s, she was teaching about 12 children and had gained a reputation as an excellent educator. That same year, the Bray Associates, a group interested in the religious education of African-American children, opened a school in Williamsburg, Virginia, for that purpose. They asked Wager to be schoolmistress, and for 14 years she taught free and enslaved African-American children reading and writing.

GLOSSARY

apprenticeship (uh-PREN-tis-ship) A period in which a young person works with an experienced person to learn a skill or trade.

astray (uh-STRAY) Away from goodness or from what is right.

blessedness (BLEH-sed-nes) Holiness or worthy of being held in great honor.

hornbook (HORN-buk) A book that was once used to teach children to read.

misbehaving (mis-bih-HAYV-ing) Acting badly or in improper ways.

needlework (NEE-del-wurk) Work that is done with a needle, like sewing or embroidery.

penmanship (PEN-man-ship) Handwriting or practicing writing with a pen.

psalm (SAHM) A sacred poem or song.

rote (ROHT) A way of learning by doing something time after time, without thinking about it.

sampler (SAM-pler) A piece of cloth on which examples of different sewing skills are stitched.

silversmith (SIL-ver-smith) Someone who makes objects from silver.

sums (SUMZ) Arithmetic problems.

tutor (TOO-ter) Someone who teaches one student or a small group of students.

venison (VEH-nuh-sun) Meat from a deer.

INDEX

A

Albemarle Parish, Virginia, 22
apprenticeship, 3, 17, 19

B

Boston, Massachusetts, 19
Boston Latin School, 22
Bray Associates, 22

C

Cheever, Ezekiel, 22

D

dame school, 3, 6, 8, 14

G

grammar school, 3, 17
Greek, 3

H

hornbook, 11
housewifery, 3

J

Jefferson, Thomas, 22

L

Latin, 3, 22

M

Madison, James, 22
Maury, James, 22
Maury School for Boys, 22
Monroe, James, 22

N

needlework, 18
New Haven, Connecticut, 22

P

penmanship, 16, 18

S

sampler, 3, 18, 19

W

Wager, Ann, 22
Williamsburg, Virginia, 22

WEBSITES

Due to the changing nature of Internet links, PowerKids Press has developed an online list of websites related to the subject of this book. This site is updated regularly. Please use this link to access the list:

www.powerkidslinks.com/jgca/teach/